Helping Children See Jesus

ISBN: 978-1-93320658-5

IN THE BEGINNING
*Creation and Man's Fall
Old Testament Volume 1
Genesis, Part 1*

Author: Arlene Piepgrass
Illustrator: Vernon Henkel
Computer Graphic Artist: Andrew Cross
Typesetting and Layout: Morgan Melton, Patricia Pope

© 2018 Bible Visuals International
PO Box 153, Akron, PA 17501-0153
Phone: (717) 859-1131
www.biblevisuals.org

All rights reserved. No part of this publication may be reproduced, stored in a retrieval system or transmitted in any form by any means, electronic, mechanical, photocopy, recording or otherwise, without the prior permission of the publisher, except as provided by USA copyright law.

RELATED ITEMS

To access related items (such as activities, memory verse posters and translated texts) please visit our web store at www.biblevisuals.org and enter 2001 at the top right of the web page. You may need to reduce the zoom setting to get the search box.

FREE TEXT DOWNLOAD

To obtain a FREE printable copy of the English teaching text (PDF format) under Product Format, please scroll down and select Extra–PDF Teacher Text Download. Then under Language select English before clicking the ADD TO CART button to place in your shopping cart. Other languages are available at an additional cost from the Language menu. When checking out, use coupon code XTACSV17 at checkout and click on Apply Coupon to receive the discount on the English text.

A

B

In the beginning God created the heaven and the earth.

Genesis 1:1

© Bible Visuals International Inc

Wherefore, as by one man sin entered into the world, and death by sin; and so death passed upon all men, for that all have sinned.

Romans 5:12

Lesson 1
IN THE BEGINNING: CREATION

Scripture to be studied: Genesis 1:1-2:7; all verses in the lesson.

The *aim* of the lesson: To show where the world and man came from.

What your students should *know*: That all of God's Word is true–including the records of how things began.

What your students should *feel*: A desire to know God who created them and to obey Him.

What your students should *do*: Believe the truth of God about the creation of mankind.

Lesson outline (for the teacher's and students' notebooks):
1. What God created (Genesis 1:1-2:7).
2. What God made known about Himself (Psalm 90:2; 104:5-9; 139:14).
3. What God provided for rest (Genesis 2:1-3).
4. What God expects of us (Psalm 148).

The verse to be memorized:

In the beginning God created the heaven and the earth.
(Genesis 1:1)

NOTE TO THE TEACHER

The opening chapters of Genesis are filled with tremendous truths. Study them carefully and prayerfully. These are from God Himself. Remember that, always!

If you have mature students, there may be some who have been taught the theory of evolution. If so, be well prepared to prove from the Word of God that He created all things.

The lessons as given here are simply suggestions. They are meant to help you. However, each lesson must be your own. Study it from the Word of God. Make sure it is true to the Word. What you yourself learn must be warmed in your heart and taught from your heart.

There are any number of ways that you may prefer to introduce the first lesson. A missionary in Taiwan (Mrs. Frances Ayton) has an excellent idea. She discusses the emptiness and darkness of earth as it was at first, contrasted with its beauty now. She talks about God and who He is. She mentions His desire to have someone with whom to share His love. Before a baby comes, its mother prepares clothing, a bed and whatever it will need. So before God made man, He had to prepare a place for him. Each day of creation is then discussed in relation to how this helps man. God gave us day so we can work and play, and night so we can rest. This idea is used through each day of creation. Finally, when everything was all prepared, God made man.

By using this suggestion, there is opportunity for student participation–which is always good.

THE LESSON

"The Bible is like a letter to you. It is from a very special Person, the God of this great universe in which you live. In the Bible, God tells you a lot of things about yourself, about Himself, about the world in which you live, about things that happened in the past and about things which will happen in the future. But most important, in the Bible God tells you about His love for people. So the Bible is really God's love letter to you"–Charles C. Ryrie, *The Young Christian's Introduction to the Bible* (Miracle Press).

God also tells us how we can know Him and how we can become members of His family. If we want to know God's message to us, we must open the Bible and study it.

Of all the books in the world, the Bible is the most marvelous. Forty different men wrote the 66 books of the Bible. Many of them never met each other for the last book was written 1,600 years after the first book. Yet all agree in everything they wrote. Though there were many men who wrote the Bible, there is only one Author, God. God, who knows everything, planned the Bible and guided each of the human writers so that each wrote without contradicting the other. (See 2 Peter 1:21.) It is God who made one Book out of the 66 books.

God cannot lie (Titus 1:2). Psalm 93:5 says, "Thy testimonies are very sure." So we know that all He tells us in the Bible is true. We can believe everything God has written to us in His Word.

Let us begin with the first book of the Bible to hear God's message to us. The title of this book is *Genesis* and it means "beginning." God used a man named Moses to write this book.

1. WHAT GOD CREATED
Genesis 1:1-2:7

As you look at the world around you, have you ever wondered where the first tree came from? Or the first flower? Or dog? Or fish? Have you wondered how the sun and moon got into the sky? Or where the first man and woman came from? Maybe you have even wondered where God came from.

God knew we would wonder about these things. So He tells us in Genesis how everything that had a beginning began.

The very first verse in the Bible, Genesis 1:1, says, "In the beginning *God* created the heaven and the earth." Out of nothing, God made the heaven and the earth.

Have you ever made anything? (Let students name things they have made.) Did you make it out of nothing? What did you need to make it? (Discuss.) God didn't need anything. He simply spoke and the heaven and earth came into being. (See Hebrews 11:3.)

Will you close your eyes, please? Are they shut tight? What do you see? Nothing? At first that is the way the earth was. There was nothing here. All was darkness and silence. So the first day God spoke and made light (Genesis 1:3-4). From then on there were day and night (Genesis 1:5).

The next day, God spoke again. He made the sky with the clouds in it. He separated the sky above from the oceans beneath it (Genesis 1:6-8).

The whole world was covered with water. So on the third day God made dry land. Then there were earth and sea. God spoke again and commanded grass to grow, flowers to bloom, trees to appear, and all the plants we know to come into being. He made them with seeds so there would be more flowers, trees and plants. How beautiful the earth was becoming! And God was pleased with everything (Genesis 1:10, 12).

Then God created the sun to shine in the day and the moon and stars to shine at night. These are time markers, marking days and years and seasons exactly as God planned (Genesis 1:14).

Did you ever try to count the stars? How many do you think God put in the sky? (Let students discuss.) No one knows the exact number of stars for there are many, many which cannot be seen. God alone knows how many stars there are. He even knows their names! (See Psalm 147:4).

Four days of God's creation were completed, and He was pleased with everything. Each day the earth and the sky were becoming more beautiful.

On the fifth day God said, "Let the seas be filled with life!" Immediately the waters were filled with all kinds of fish. (Name fish familiar to your area.) Then God spoke again, saying, "Let the skies be filled with life!" Instantly, birds of all kinds were chirping and flying everywhere. The robins, sparrows, pigeons, parrots, bluejays (mention your local birds) were all created that day. And God saw that everything was good. (See Genesis 1:20-22.)

But God was not finished. Do you have animals at home? What kind? (Let students name them.) The sixth day, God created all kinds of animals. He created dogs and cats, lions and tigers, elephants and mice. All the animals were created by God that day (Genesis 1:24-25).

God had a special commandment for the birds, fish and animals. "Be fruitful and multiply," He said. This meant that robins would have baby robins, fish would have baby fish, dogs would have puppies.

We have talked about the beginning of everything around us. But where did the first man come from?

God said "We need someone to be in charge of all the animals, birds and fish which We have created. We need someone to care for the ground. We need someone who can love Us and talk to Us." So God took some dust of the ground and made the first man. Then He breathed His own life into the man's nostrils. Think of it–life from God! Immediately the man was alive! God called the first man *Adam*, which means "dust."

God created Adam "in his own image" (Genesis 1:27). Adam had the power to know, to understand, to choose and to love. Adam was intelligent–much more intelligent than any of the animals God had created.

God brought all the animals to Adam, and Adam gave them names. Have you ever tried to name anything? That's hard! Adam was smart! God said to Adam, "You are the master over all the animals I have created."

Because Adam was created in the image of God, he was able to talk to God and to love God. He could make choices and decisions. God knew Adam needed a companion. No animal was suitable because none was created in the image of God and for that reason could not worship God. That is the difference between animals and people. People can know and worship God; animals cannot. God caused Adam to fall sound asleep and then He took part of Adam's side and made a wife for him.

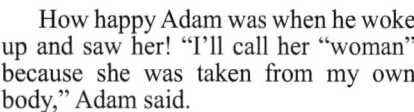

Show Illustration #1

How happy Adam was when he woke up and saw her! "I'll call her "woman" because she was taken from my own body," Adam said.

And that was the way the first family began.

2. WHAT GOD MADE KNOWN ABOUT HIMSELF
Psalm 90:2; 104:5-9; 139:14

From creation we learn that GOD IS ETERNAL.

Maybe you are wondering, "But where did God come from?" Let's look at the first verse in the Bible again. Genesis 1:1 says, "In the beginning God created the heaven and the earth." Before there was anything else, God lived. He was there even before He created the stars, the sun, the world, or anything (Psalm 90:2). God never had a beginning, and He will never have an ending. He is "from everlasting to everlasting." We cannot understand this but we know it is true because God says so and He cannot lie.

From creation we learn that GOD IS POWERFUL.

Simply by speaking, God was able to bring into being everything we see around us. He was able to give life to plants and animals. Then He made Adam and Eve like Himself so they could think and love and talk with Him.

God created the oceans, and He keeps them in their boundaries so they will never again cover the whole earth (Psalm 104:5-9).

God not only put the stars, moon and sun in the sky, but He keeps them there (Hebrews 1:3). God has all power!

From creation we learn that He is ALL-WISE.

Show Illustration #2A

Think about the sun. Our wise God knew exactly how close to the earth the sun had to be to make us warm. If He had placed it closer, we would burn up–just as we would if we stood too close to a fire. If God had placed the sun farther from the earth, we would freeze to death.

Think of the air we breathe. In His wisdom God put in the air exactly what we need (oxygen) to keep us alive.

Show Illustration #2B

Look at your body. You can feel, smell, see and hear because the God of wisdom made you that way. He gave you hands with which to do things, fingers to hold things, feet to take you places. Your heart beats to keep you alive without your even thinking about it. Your eyes blink automatically to keep dust and dirt from flying into them. You are "fearfully and wonderfully made" (Psalm 139:14).

3. WHAT GOD PROVIDED FOR REST
Genesis 2:1-3

On the evening of the sixth day, God looked over all He had created and saw it was very good. On the seventh day, God rested (Genesis 2:3). In His wisdom God knew we would need regular times to rest so He set an example for us.

Show Illustration #3

God gives us six days to work and one day to rest and to worship Him. He loves us and knows what is best for us.

When we work every day without taking one day to rest, we rob God of honor and worship. We also rob ourselves, for our bodies become weak. We lose the joy of serving and obeying God.

4. WHAT GOD EXPECTS OF US
Psalm 148
Show Illustration #4

Some people teach that the first man came out of a hole in the ground. Others think he developed from a fish. Many teach that man evolved from a monkey. (Refer to whatever myth is believed by the people of your area.) These are Satan's lies about creation. God tells us in His Word that He made man "in His own image." He expects us to believe His Word. Do you choose to believe the truth of God or the lies of Satan?

Since God is your Creator, He expects you to know what He is like and what He has done for you. He expects you to obey Him. To know Him and to obey Him, you must study His Word, the Bible.

God has the right to tell us how to live because He made us. All of God's creation is commanded to praise Him (Psalm 148). That includes you and me. Have you ever thanked Him for all the beauty He has made? Have you thanked Him for giving you life? You praise and thank Him most by believing what He says is true.

Lesson 2
THE BEGINNING OF SIN

Scripture to be studied: Genesis 2:8-3:24 and all verses in the lesson.

The *aim* of the lesson: To show how sin entered the world and how God judged sin.

What your students should *know*: That Satan is the author of sin.

What your students should *feel*: A hatred for sin.

What your students should *do*: Accept God's provision for pardon from sin.

Lesson outline (for the teacher's and students' notebooks):
1. A perfect home (Genesis 2:8-25).
2. A disobedient act (Genesis 3:1-7).
3. A severe judgment (Genesis 3:8-19, 23-24).
4. A loving provision (Genesis 3:21).

The verse to be memorized:

Wherefore, as by one man sin entered into the world, and death by sin; and so death passed upon all men, for that all have sinned. (Romans 5:12)

THE LESSON

> **NOTE TO THE TEACHER**
>
> Your students must see at once the awfulness of sin. God is holy; He is pure. He will not, cannot, tolerate sin. If your group is untaught in the Word of God, spend much time in concluding the lesson. Help them to see that alongside the holiness of God and His hatred for sin is His love. Because He loves us, He Himself (in the person of His Son) has provided a substitute for our sins.
>
> Study carefully the notes on the inside back cover of this volume.

Is everything perfect where you live? Do you ever have any problems? Is there always complete joy and happiness in your home? Do you ever lack anything you need? Today we are going to learn about a perfect home. We are also going to learn why *your* home is not perfect.

1. A PERFECT HOME
Genesis 2:8-25

How God loved Adam whom He created in His own image! How He loved Eve, the woman He made from Adam's body!

In Eden, God provided a beautiful garden for Adam and Eve to live in. It was the most beautiful garden there ever was, with every kind of tree. Many of the trees had delicious fruit. There were no worms or diseases to spoil the fruit so none was ever rotten. How good the garden must have smelled with all the blossoms of the trees and all the flowers blooming everywhere!

Show Illustration #5

A cool, refreshing river watered the garden. Adam and Eve enjoyed watching the birds and animals. All this was lovely. But even more enjoyable were God's evening visits. How they enjoyed telling Him about the day!

Once God said, "Adam, I want you to take care of the garden for Me. You are master over all the birds and animals here. You may eat all the fruit you want except the fruit of one tree." Stopping at a tree in the middle of the garden, God continued, "Adam, do you see this tree?"

Adam nodded.

"This is the 'tree of the knowledge of good and evil.' You must *never* eat the fruit from this tree. It is the only fruit you must not eat." God warned, "If you disobey Me and eat this fruit, you will surely die! Adam, I want you to obey me."

Surely Adam and Eve would never want to take any fruit from that tree! They didn't need it. They had mangoes, oranges, apples, plums (or name fruits your students are familiar with)–all they could eat or want. Surely they would want to obey God who had provided such a magnificent place for them to live.

Each day was a happy day. They were never sick. They were never sad. They never cried They were never afraid. They were never angry. Everything was perfect.

They didn't know that God had an enemy called Satan. They didn't know that Satan was jealous of God and that he didn't want them to obey God. A long time before, Satan had been a beautiful angel in Heaven. But then he sinned and was forced out of Heaven. Now he hated God and he hated all that God did.

The Bible doesn't tell us what Satan thought as he saw Adam and Eve in God's perfect garden. It may have been like this:

God does not want them to eat of the tree of the knowledge of good and evil because He doesn't want them to know about

- 21 -

me. He doesn't want them to be on my side. If I can make them eat that fruit, maybe I can get them on my side against God.

2. A DISOBEDIENT ACT
Genesis 3:1-7

Satan looked over all the creatures God had created. He chose the most beautiful of all, the serpent, to use as his body. At that time, the serpent did not crawl but was upright and moved gracefully.

One day as Eve was strolling through the garden, the serpent came up to her and began to talk. She enjoyed having someone to talk to. And, since there was nothing to be afraid of, Eve had no fear. She didn't know that the one who was talking through the serpent was the enemy of God.

Show Illustration #6

"Eve," Satan began. "You certainly don't mean to say that God will not let you eat of *every* tree in the garden." Satan wanted Eve to become dissatisfied with God. He wanted her to think that God was denying her something good.

"God said we may eat of every tree except one," Eve replied. "He told us that if we eat that fruit or even touch it, we will die."

Oh, Eve was not telling the exact truth! God hadn't told them not to touch it, only not to eat it. God had said they would *surely* die if they ate the fruit of that tree.

Satan quickly responded, "Eve, you won't die if you eat of that tree. God knows that if you eat the fruit from the tree of the knowledge of good and evil you will know as much as He does. You will be wise. *Now* you know only what is good; but *then* you could know evil as well."

Satan made it sound as if it would be better to know good *and* evil. What a lie that was! How much better it was to know only good.

Eve walked over to the tree to take a closer look. She thought, *The fruit does look good. It really is beautiful. I wonder if it really would make me wise?*

Eve had to make a choice. God had given her and Adam the ability to make choices. *Shall I try it?* She wondered. *God told us not to eat it. But if it will make me wise, I think I will try it.*

Eve reached up, plucked some of the fruit and ate it. She deliberately disobeyed her Creator's command.

Turning to Adam, she said, "Adam, taste this fruit! It's from the tree of knowledge of good and evil. It's delicious! It will make us wise. The serpent told me not to be afraid to eat it. He said we will not surely die. Take a bite."

Now Adam had a choice to make. He knew God had commanded him not to eat this fruit. But he didn't want to lose Eve. He'd been lonely without her. So he took the fruit Eve offered him and ate it. This was rebellious disobedience.

Both Adam and Eve chose to listen to Satan and disobey God. This was sin. Satan gained a victory. He introduced sin into that beautiful garden and into those perfect lives which God had created in His image. Oh, what a sad day that was! The moment they disobeyed the command of God, Adam and Eve became sinners.

Yes, Adam and Eve now knew good and evil. They knew, too, that what they had done was evil. They were UNHAPPY because of their sin.

They looked at themselves and realized they were uncovered. They felt naked before God. They felt GUILTY because of their sin. Quickly they gathered leaves from the trees and sewed them together to cover their bodies.

Suddenly they heard God. Before this they had looked forward to His visit. Today was different. They were AFRAID to meet God because of their sin.

"Adam, Adam, where are you?" God called.

"I am hiding," answered Adam. "I heard You coming and I was afraid. I am naked and I did not want You to see me."

"Adam, who said you were naked? Did you eat of the tree that I told you not to?" God questioned.

"It was not really my fault." Adam replied. "The woman You gave me picked the fruit and game me some to taste."

God asked Eve, "What have you done?"

"It was not my fault," Eve replied. "The serpent made me take some and eat it."

It was easy for each one to blame another. Both Adam and Eve could have chosen to say "no" to Satan. But both chose to disobey God. Both could have said to God, "I disobeyed You and I am sorry." But instead both said, "It was not my fault."

3. A SEVERE JUDGMENT
Genesis 3:8-19, 23-24

That was a sad day for God. Because He is holy and just (Deuteronomy 32:4), He had to punish Adam and Eve. They had disobeyed Him and He could not close His eyes to their sin.

God turned first to the serpent saying, "Because you let Satan use your body, you will crawl in the dust and eat dust from now on." (Did God do what He said? How do snakes move about?)

Show Illustration #7

To Eve, God said, "You will have many sorrows. When your children are born, you will have much pain. Your husband will be your master to rule over you."

Speaking to Adam, God said, "Adam, you knew you were not allowed to eat the fruit from the tree of the knowledge of good and evil. I commanded you not to and you understood. You've enjoyed taking care of this beautiful garden. It hasn't been hard. Everything has grown easily and produced lots of fruit. But, from now on, things will be different. In the place where you'll be living, there'll be thorns and thistles and all kinds of weeds. You'll have to work hard to make trees bear fruit and to make food grow. You'll perspire; your back will hurt; your hands will get blisters.

"And Adam, you will die and your body will become dust again, just like it was before I created you and gave you life."

Adam and Eve had never been sad before this day. Now for the first time, they cried. They knew they had caused God, whom they loved, to be sad. Their own sin had ruined their friendship with God and their happy life in the garden.

"Adam," God continued, "you and your wife will have to leave the garden."

What a sad, sad day! No longer would Adam and Eve be able to walk through the garden with God in the evening. God is holy (Psalm 22:3). He cannot overlook sin (Isaiah 59:2).

4. A LOVING PROVISION
Genesis 3:21

But before God forced Adam and Eve out of the garden, He showed them He still loved them. He showed them how they could again worship Him and talk to Him.

God killed some animals, letting the blood pour out on the ground. Using the skins of the animals, He made clothes for Adam and Eve. The Bible doesn't tell us what God said to them as He did this, but it may have been something like this:

"Adam, these animals are innocent. They did not disobey Me. *You* are the one who sinned. Because sin must be punished, I killed these animals in your place. I have made these clothes for you from their skins. Their blood was shed for you. You now know the difference between good and evil. You will often choose to do evil. From now on, when you come to worship Me you must kill an animal as a sacrifice for your sins. Blood must be shed before you can come to Me." (See Hebrews 9:22.)

God continued, "But, Adam, you can be certain that when you obey Me by bringing a sacrifice, I will hear your prayer and forgive your sin. I still love you, Adam. I am giving you another chance to obey Me."

God added: "Satan tempted you to sin. He thinks he has defeated Me. But he's wrong." Then He gave them a wonderful promise: "One day, my Son, the Lord Jesus Christ, will die on the cross for your sins and the sins of everyone in the world. Then Satan will be defeated." (This is the meaning of Genesis 3:15.)

As Adam and Eve sadly left the garden, God placed His angel at the entrance. Adam and Eve would never be able to return. But they could still talk to God in prayer if they would come to Him with a sacrifice as He commanded.

Adam and Eve were the very first parents of all of us. The verse we have been memorizing tells us that because they sinned, we too are sinners. God does not change. Just as their sin had to be punished, so must ours. (See Romans 6:23.)

God is still holy. He cannot tolerate sin. Just as their sin separated them from God, so does ours.

Show Illustration #8

Almost 2,000 years ago God did send His Son into the world just as He had promised so long before. Jesus Christ died on the cross for our sins. He was the perfect sacrifice who shed His blood so we can live.

When you believe this, He forgives your sin forever and gives you eternal life (John 3:16). Do you believe the Lord Jesus is the Son of God? Do you know you are a sinner? Do you believe that Jesus died in your place for your sin? If you do, will you ask Him to forgive you and to come into your heart and life?

Lesson 3
THE BEGINNING OF FAMILY LIFE

Scripture to be studied: Genesis 3:16-4:26; verses cited in the lesson.

The *aim* of the lesson: To show that the only way to come to God is through the blood of the Lamb.

What your students should *know*: That God punished sin but provides forgiveness through the Lamb of God.

What your students should *feel*: A fear of coming to God any way but God's way.

What your students should *do*: Accept the sacrifice of Christ on the cross and receive forgiveness for all their sins.

Lesson outline (for the teacher's and students' notebooks):
1. Life outside the garden (Genesis 3:16-4:2).
2. Spiritual training in the home (Genesis 4:3-5).
3. Obedience or rebellion (Genesis 4:6-10).
4. The man God could not save (Genesis 4:11-16).

The verse to be memorized:

Wherefore, as by one man sin entered into the world, and death by sin; and so death passed upon all men, for that all have sinned. (Romans 5:12)

NOTE TO THE TEACHER

Ask God to reveal to you something simple to illustrate the substitutionary work of Christ. He, the perfect Lamb of God, took the place of every sinner. He took upon Himself the sins of all. He took the punishment for those sins. If you know of an animal that protected its young and, in doing so, died, relate it to your students. Perhaps someone was drowning. Another jumped in to rescue him; and the rescuer lost his life while the one who had been drowning was saved. Help your students to understand the glorious truth of Christ's becoming our substitute. (See Isaiah 53:6.)

THE LESSON
1. LIFE OUTSIDE THE GARDEN
Genesis 3:16-4:2

Life for Adam and Eve was suddenly changed when they listened to Satan and disobeyed God. Now they no longer enjoyed the security of the beautiful garden of Eden where they had walked and talked with God. No longer could they simply trim the trees and enjoy the fruit.

Instead, their daily work was difficult. The ground was hard and dry. Weeds grew easily. The seeds they planted grew slowly. Worms got into the fruit on the trees. Disease made plants and trees die. Adam and Eve became tired. They felt discouraged. Sometimes they were sick.

The Bible does not tell us what they talked about at the end of the day's work, but it might have been something like this:

"Adam," Eve began, "if only we had obeyed God. If only I hadn't listened to Satan's voice and eaten that fruit. How different things would be for us!"

"Eve, my dear, it's too late to change what we did. We must thank God that He has provided a way for us to talk with Him even though we have sinned. Think of it; we may kill an animal as a sacrifice for our sin. We must be thankful that He forgives our sin and still loves us and cares for us," Adam said comfortingly. And Eve was thankful.

Together, Adam and Eve obeyed God. But when they did wrong things, they brought sacrifices so God would forgive them. They knew what was good and what was bad. But sometimes they chose to do what was wrong. They got angry. They argued. They grumbled. How do we know they did these sinful things? They were like us–and this is the way we act!

One day a baby boy was born into their family. Adam and Eve named him Cain. He was the very first *baby*. (God had created Adam and Eve as *adults*.)

Show Illustration #9

Later Cain had a baby brother. Adam and Eve named him Abel. These two brought much joy into that home. But they brought sadness, too. For both boys were sinners like their parents. They had received sin natures. They screamed when they could not have their own way. They hit each other. They were exactly like you! Adam and Eve's sins were now being seen in the lives of their children.

2. SPIRITUAL TRAINING IN THE HOME
Genesis 4:3-5

Talking with his wife one day, Adam said, "Eve, we must teach these boys about God. We must tell them about all that God created. We must tell them about the garden in Eden. We must explain why we are living outside the garden. They too are sinners. We must teach them how their sins can be forgiven so they can worship God."

Adam taught his sons how to plant gardens. He taught them how to take care of the animals. But more important, he taught them they were sinners. He explained that God hates sin. He told them that the only way they could worship God and have forgiveness of sin was through a sacrifice.

Cain and Abel often went with their father to choose an animal for a sacrifice.

Cain asked his father, "Why don't you use that skinny little lamb over there? He wouldn't be good to eat. Let's give that one to God."

"Oh, no, my son!" Adam answered. "Only the best is good enough for God. He loves us and is willing to forgive our sins. He won't make us die for our sins. He will accept the blood of this innocent lamb in our place. We want to give Him the best of the flock."

Cain and Abel saw the angel guarding the entrance of the garden of Eden. This helped them to understand that God hates sin. They watched their parents offer the sacrifice. They saw how happy their parents were when God accepted their offering and forgave their sins.

As Cain grew to be a young man, he became a farmer. He enjoyed digging in the earth and planting seeds. He watched as the plants grew and produced fruit and vegetables.

Abel loved animals. He cared for them–especially the baby animals. He tended the flocks.

Show Illustration #10

The boys began to understand, too, that they were sinners. They each had to bring a sacrifice to God if they wanted forgiveness of sin. Simply watching their parents offer sacrifices was not enough. (See Hebrews 11:4.)

3. OBEDIENCE OR REBELLION
Genesis 4:6-10

As Cain walked through his gardens one day, he thought, *This fruit is beautiful. Why should I give an animal sacrifice? Instead of killing an animal, I will give my fruit to God for a sacrifice. I like my way better.* (See Proverbs 14:12.)

Would this please God? *(No)* Why not? (Let students discuss. Lead them to conclude that this was disobedience and rebellion against God.)

As Abel looked over his flock he thought to himself, *I must find the best lamb to offer to God. It must not be sick or have any spots.*

When Cain and Abel offered their sacrifices on the altar, God accepted Abel's lamb. But He did not accept Cain's fruit. God loved Cain as much as He loved Abel. Both boys were sinners. Both knew how to worship God and receive forgiveness of sin. But only one obeyed God's command.

Cain became very angry when he saw that God refused his sacrifice! "Why are you so angry, Cain?" God asked. "You know you must kill an animal and offer it to Me if you want your sins forgiven. Get a lamb. Kill it and offer it. I will accept it just as I accepted Abel's. Your sins will also be forgiven."

What a loving God! He wanted Cain to obey Him.

But Cain was stubborn. He wanted his own way instead of God's way. He became jealous of Abel because God had accepted his lamb (1 John 3:12). He thought, *I'll get even with him!*

The more he thought about it, the more he hated Abel. His hatred grew and grew. One day he said to Abel, "Let's go for a walk."

They walked and talked for a long time. Then, when he was certain no one could see them, Cain killed Abel.

Show Illustration #11

No one saw me. No one will know what happened, Cain thought.

Cain had forgotten one thing. God could see him all the time. "Where is your brother, Abel?" God asked.

"I don't know. How should I know where he is?" Cain answered.

How easily one sin leads to another! Cain disobeyed God. He became angry when God scolded him. He became jealous of Abel for obeying God. So he killed Abel. And he lied to God.

4. THE MAN GOD COULD NOT SAVE
Genesis 4:11-16

"I saw what you did, Cain," God said. "I saw your brother's blood on the ground. Cain, from now on the ground will not produce fruits and vegetables for you as it did. Even when you cultivate it and plant seeds, your harvest will not be plentiful."

If Cain had said, "O God, I've done wrong and I'm sorry. Will you forgive me? I will obey You. I will offer a lamb for my sins!" God would have forgiven him.

Show Illustration #12

But instead, Cain refused to say he was sorry. He pitied himself and cried to God saying, "My punishment is too great. I cannot stand it. I will be like a tramp on the earth. Everyone will try to kill me."

"No, they will not kill you, Cain. I'll put a mark on you so you will be protected," God replied. Cain didn't deserve the protection of God. But God is slow to anger. He "is long-suffering, not willing that any should perish, but that all should come to repentance" (2 Peter 3:9).

Cain was sorry that he had been caught. He was sorry he was going to be punished. He was not sorry he had sinned and disobeyed God. He chose to go his own way (Genesis 4:16).

What a sad day! What a terrible decision to make! God wanted to forgive Cain. But He could not because Cain would not ask God to forgive him. Instead, Cain went farther and farther away from God. He built a city for his children and got busy with music and industry so he could forget God.

Cain never did repent. When he died, God could not receive him into His presence to live with Him forever. Instead, Cain was sent to eternal punishment, forever separated from God.

Adam and Eve were sad because of Cain's disobedience. They were distressed because Abel was killed. Abel loved God.

"Adam," Eve asked, "do you remember the promise God gave us in the garden?" He said He would send Someone to defeat Satan. How will this be possible now that Abel is dead and Cain refuses to obey God?"

God answered this question for Eve by giving to them another baby boy whom they named Seth. He grew up to obey God. Many thousands of years later, God's Son, the Lord Jesus Christ, was born to Seth's descendants. God kept His promise (Luke 2:7; 3:38).

Today there are many people like Cain. They won't be saved because they don't listen to God's Word or obey His commands. There is still only one way to come to God. His Son, Jesus Christ, shed His blood on the cross for our sins. Jesus Himself said He is the only way to come to God (John 14:6). No other name under Heaven can save us (Acts 4:12).

Some people think that if they join a church, God will forgive their sins. Some people feel that God will forgive their sins because they were baptized. Some people think that if their parents were Christians, they too will go to Heaven when they die. These things are good and proper if one *has* believed. But they are no substitutes for faith in the Lord Jesus Christ.

God's Word is final. He means what He says. And He says, "Believe on the Lord Jesus Christ, and you will be saved." Christ shed His blood so you can have forgiveness of sin and eternal life. Will you come to God His way and let Him save you?

Lesson 4
THE JUDGMENT OF GOD

Scripture to be studied: Genesis 6:1–9:29; all verses appearing in lesson.

The *aim* of the lesson: To show that the judgment of God is sure and terrible.

What your students should *know*: What God promises, He will do.

What your students should *feel*: A desire to be "in Christ."

What your students should *do*: Accept the safety offered by God in Christ.

Lesson outline (for the teacher's and students' notebooks):

1. God sees everyone always (Genesis 6:1-12).
2. God decided to destroy (Genesis 6:13).
3. The plan of God for saving Noah (Genesis 6:14-22).
4. The judgment of God (Genesis 7:1–9:29).

The verse to be memorized:

Wherefore, as by one man sin entered into the world, and death by sin; and so death passed upon all men, for that all have sinned. (Romans 5:12)

NOTE TO THE TEACHER

It is imperative that your students understand that God means what He says. They must see that there is no way of coming to God except His way. Emphasize the truth of the verse we have been memorizing. All who have not believed in the Lord Jesus Christ and placed their trust in Him are already condemned. This is serious! Do all you can to help them to see the importance of turning to the Saviour.

THE LESSON

Did you ever do something bad, thinking nobody saw you? God saw you. Maybe it was dark or you were alone. God still saw you! Maybe you think, *Nothing has happened to me. I did not get caught.* But God saw you and God punishes evil, as we will see in today's lesson.

1. GOD SEES EVERYONE ALWAYS
Genesis 6:1-12

When God created the earth with the animals, birds and people, He looked at it and saw that it was all very good. God was pleased with His creation (Genesis 1:31). But then, something dreadful happened. Adam and Eve sinned. Now as God looked at His creation, He saw sin had spoiled His perfect work.

The children Adam and Eve had were sinners like their parents. Each was born with a sin nature. What a sad day for all of them when Cain murdered his brother! This was a result of sin. Once again Adam and Eve thought, *Oh, if only we had obeyed God!*

Adam and Eve had more children, boys and girls (Genesis 5:4). Each one of them was a sinner. Adam and Eve had grandchildren and they were sinners just as their parents and grandparents were. Some of them obeyed God and offered sacrifices for their sins as God had commanded them. This pleased God. But most of them forgot God and chose their own way.

Time went on for more than 1,500 years. That is a long time. The population of the earth grew rapidly. The more sinners there were, the more evil there was, and the worse things became.

People thought they were happy. They had parties; they had weddings; they worked; they played. Life was much like we know it today. (See Matthew 24:37-38.) Crime and violence were common. People were selfish. They hurt others to get what they wanted. Their thoughts were wicked. They hated. They lied. They cheated. They murdered. (See Genesis 6:11.)

Show Illustration #13

Only one family was different from all the others. In this family were a father named Noah, a mother and three sons. The three sons were Shem, Ham and Japheth.

Noah knew he was a sinner. He knew God hates sin. His father and grandfather had taught him this and he believed them. He taught his three sons that they were sinners. He regularly killed an animal and offered it as a sacrifice to God so that God would forgive his sins. And as God saw Noah offer the blood of the animal and repent of his sins, He forgave him.

2. GOD DECIDES TO DESTROY
Genesis 6:13

Show Illustration #14

Looking down on all the sin, God said, "I'm sorry I created men. They are wicked. All their thoughts are wicked and hateful. All their actions are bad. It makes me sad to see people disobeying Me.

"Noah is the only one who offers sacrifices to Me. He is the only one who admits he is a sinner and asks Me to forgive his sins. All the others act as if I do not exist. I'm going to show them that I do exist. I'll destroy everything and every person on the earth–everyone except Noah and his family."

3. THE PLAN OF GOD FOR SAVING NOAH
Genesis 6:14-22

God told Noah about His plans. "Noah, I'm going to destroy every living person on the earth. They've become very wicked. They refuse to repent of their sins. They refuse to ask Me to forgive them. I created them to love and serve Me. Instead, they live for themselves and serve Satan.

"I'm going to cover the whole world with a deep, deep flood. Every man, woman, child and animal will be drowned in the flood. But, Noah, because you have obeyed Me, I am going to keep you and your wife and your three sons and their wives alive through the flood. You will be saved.

"Listen carefully, Noah, because I'm going to give you the instructions for building a large ship."

Noah listened carefully as God told him to make the boat 450 feet long, 75 feet wide, and 45 feet high. (*Teacher:* Compare size with some building your students know.)

"You must cover it inside and outside with pitch so not a drop of water will be able to get in," God instructed. "Make a window all the way around the ship, eighteen inches below the roof so you will have light and air. Make three decks in the boat and build rooms and stalls on the decks. And, Noah, I want you to put a door in the side of the boat."

God was specific with His instructions. And Noah gave attention to every detail. He realized that His life and the lives of his family depended on his obedience to God's commands.

Before Noah had a chance to wonder why the boat had to be so large, God said, "Besides your family, I want you to take a pair of every kind of animal into the boat with you–a male and female. Of those which are good for eating and for sacrifices you must take seven pairs." What a zoo Noah would have with him! What quantities of food he would need to feed them all! Noah knew now why the ship had to be so big and needed many rooms.

Noah's neighbors and friends became curious as they saw him begin to build. "What are you doing there, Noah?" they asked as they stopped to watch.

"I'm building a ship," replied Noah.

"A ship!" they exclaimed. "Where do you expect to use that? There is no water around here. The ocean is far away. Even the river is only a little stream that we can wade across."

"God told me to build it," answered Noah. "God sees how wicked you are. If you do not repent of your sins, He is going to destroy you. He is going to send a flood, and you will all drown unless you repent and ask God to forgive you." So Noah preached to the curious crowds who came to see him and his sons building the ark.

Show Illustration #15

"Did you hear what he said?" they laughed. "Whoever heard of a flood? Whoever heard of rain? There's no water near us. Noah is crazy. He thinks he is so good. He's no better than we are."

Day after day Noah and his sons continued their work on the ark. Children sometimes stopped their play to watch him. "My father says you are crazy, Mr. Noah. He says God won't send a flood. He says you just made up that story."

"No, my children, I did not make up the story. God hates sin. God is very sorry your fathers refuse to offer sacrifices to Him and refuse to ask His forgiveness for their sins. God wants you to ask Him to forgive your sins. If you do, you may come into the ark with me when the floods come."

But the children laughed and ran back to their play.

"Why is your husband building that ridiculous ship?" Mrs. Noah's friends asked her.

"God has told him He's going to destroy every living person and animal on the earth. That includes you, unless you will obey Him and seek His forgiveness," Mrs. Noah answered sadly. "I wish you'd listen and obey God. If you do, you can go into the ark with us and you won't drown when the flood comes."

But no one would believe. For 120 years Noah continued to build his boat. All during that time he told the people what God was going to do. He told them how they could escape the flood. (See 1 Peter 3:20.) But no one repented. Everybody continued working, playing, eating, drinking, having parties, having weddings, having funerals as usual.

"Why should we believe Noah?" they asked. "Nothing has changed. Everything is going on as usual."

Finally the ark was finished. Again God spoke to Noah saying, "Come into the ark, you and all your family. Bring in the animals too."

In they went. Every kind of animal that was ever created went into the ship two by two, a male and a female. And there was room for all.

Again the neighbors and friends crowded around watching what was happening. They laughed among themselves, saying, "They're out of their minds! How do they expect to live in that boat?"

While they were watching, someone called, "Look! The door is closing! No one is pulling it shut. It's closing by itself. That is really strange!" (It looked as if it were closing by itself; actually, God closed the door. See Genesis 7:16.)

4. THE JUDGMENT OF GOD
Genesis 7:1–9:29

Then the rain began to fall. It just poured. Outside a little boy grabbed his father's hand crying, "I'm afraid! You told me it wouldn't rain like Noah said. You told me he was crazy."

"Don't cry, son. We'll go home. The rain won't hurt us," his father assured him. "It will soon stop."

But it didn't stop. Day after day the rain continued in torrents. The water began to cover the earth. People scrambled out of their houses and climbed to the hills. As the water continued to rise, they ran to the mountains. And still the rain continued.

"Will the rain never stop? Was Noah telling the truth?" they cried. "Noah!" they shouted. "Open the door! Please let us in!"

But God had closed the door. And it was too late for anyone else to enter.

Show Illustration #16

It continued to rain for forty days and forty nights. The water covered the mountains. Exactly as God had said, all the people drowned. But Noah and his family were safe inside the ark. All the animals were safe too. The ark simply rose with the water and floated gently.

Then one day the rain stopped. God caused a wind to blow. The waters began to dry up. The water had been so high that it took many months for it to go down. Finally, after a whole year and ten days (Genesis 7:11; 8:13-14), God said to Noah, "Today you may leave the boat. The earth is dry again. Take your family with you and take out all the animals too. Empty the ship completely. You won't need it any more."

Every person who had entered the ship came out. Every animal that had gone in came out. God kept them safe, exactly as He had promised.

Now no one was around to watch them. There was no one to laugh at them. Everyone was dead. God meant what He had said. He had warned the people that He would destroy them. And He kept His word.

Immediately Noah built an altar. He killed some birds and animals and offered them on the altar as sacrifices to God. How thankful he was that God had protected him and his family!

God was pleased that Noah remembered to thank Him and to worship Him. He gave Noah a wonderful promise, saying, "I will never again destroy the world with a flood. I will put a rainbow in the sky as a sign of My promise" (Genesis 9:9-17).

God did *not* say, "I will not punish sin again." Oh, no! Quite the opposite. He says, "It is appointed unto men once to die, but after this the judgment" (Hebrews 9:27). What kind of judgment does He mean? In Revelation 20:15 God says, "Whosoever was not found written in the book of life was cast into the lake of fire." Think of it! Spending all eternity separated from God in a lake of fire! Only those whose names are written in the Lamb's book of life will go to Heaven (Revelation 21:27).

But how do we get our names written in this book? John 3:16 tells us: "Whosoever believeth in Him [God's Son] should not perish, but have eternal life." You might say, "I do not believe that," just as Noah's neighbors said. But that will not make any difference to God. He means what He says whether you believe it or not. And He says, "He that believeth not is condemned already, because he hath not believed in the name of the only begotten Son of God" (John 3:18). And, ". . . he that believeth not the Son shall not see life; but the wrath of God abideth on him" (John 3:36).

When you obey God and believe in your heart that Jesus died on the cross for your sins, then you have eternal life. You are safe in Christ, just as Noah was safe in the ark. The judgment of God will not touch you, just as the flood did not touch Noah.

Everyone who trusts in Christ and depends on Him alone for salvation *has* eternal life. Everyone who went into the ark came out of the ark safely. Likewise, all who are "in Christ" are safe forever. (See John 10:28-29.)

Will you be like Noah and believe God and His Word? Or will you be like Noah's neighbors and be destroyed because of unbelief? You must make the choice.

www.ingramcontent.com/pod-product-compliance
Lightning Source LLC
Chambersburg PA
CBHW060804090426
42736CB00002B/151